Rick and Jane Learn to
Listen & Talk

The First Step to Intimacy

LEARN TO BE MARRIED SERIES
Al & Autumn Ray

ISBN: 145281287X
ISBN-13: 9781452812878

Library of Congress Control Number: 2010905532

Rick and Jane Learn to Listen and Talk
(The First Step to Intimacy)

Learn to Be Married Series

The couples depicted in this narrative are fictional. Any resemblance to current or past coaches or player couples is purely coincidental.

MarriageTeam
PO Box 873086
Vancouver, WA 98687-3086
(360) 450-6042
www.MarriageTeam.org

Look for all the books in the

Learn to be Married Series

<u>Coming Soon</u>

Rick and Jane Learn to

Use Anger Creatively

ENDORSEMENTS

It is short. It is simple. It is easy to read. It could change the way you talk and listen. It will also introduce you to "marriage coaching." I highly recommend it.

~ **Dr. Gary Chapman,** best-selling author of *The Five Love Languages*

Wow, this was a wonderful way to spend thirty minutes. I didn't stop reading until I had finished it, and I will definitely get copies to share with my family and friends. I love this story. Not only is it entertaining, simple and useful, it encourages positive and intentional action. What a great combination! I used to be a marriage and family counselor, and I would have loved a resource like this!

~ **Dr. Linda J. Miller**, Master Certified Coach, global liaison for coaching, The Ken Blanchard Companies

MarriageTeam is equipping real couples to coach others with the practical and understandable skills they need to "win" in their own marriages. This practical approach is reflected in this wonderful little book, Rick and Jane Learn to Listen and Talk: The First Step to Intimacy. Don't miss the life-changing truths hidden in this simple story. See Rick grow...see Jane grow!

~ **Dr. Peter Larsen**, president, Life Innovations (PREPARE/ENRICH), co-author *The Couple Check-up*

I LOVE IT!!!! In a fun and memorable way, the Ray's remind us of the basics about marriage: we all need to improve our communication and we are a team. By spending just fifteen minutes with this book, you can improve your connection with your spouse. Read it and enjoy it. You'll never forget it.

~ **Dr Steve Stephens**, licensed psychologist and author of more than twenty books with over a million copies sold

I found Rick and Jane to be an entertaining and deeply informative contribution to the field of marriage coaching. Al and Autumn's creative use of the "playbook" metaphor helps simplify the relational steps toward life-giving communication and intimacy. This is a book that every married couple can enjoy and learn practical skills to apply immediately!

~ **Jerome Daley**, ACC, DPM, Leadership Coach, publisher of
Christian Coaching Magazine and author of six books

It's not often that an author paints such a clear picture of the vision she/he has for following God's call on his/her life. In Rick and Jane Learn to Listen and Talk, Alan and Autumn Ray have done just that with clear and simple language about the marriage relationship – and the ways we communicate (or don't!). In this easy-to-read book, the reader will find practical and honest answers (and most importantly, questions) to help communicate with their spouse. I think every pastor will want this resource on his/her bookshelf.

~ **Bill Copper**, director, Hollifield Leadership Center

As a former NFL quarterback, I love the concept of marriage coaching. This book demonstrates what so many couples need these days…the basic communication and coaching help that keeps a husband and wife on the same team. The basics of communication are crucial, and most all of us need help to practice them. This book shows us how.

~ **Jeff Kemp**, president, Stronger Families and senior fellow,
Marriage and Family Foundation

The MarriageTeam has put together a practical, fast read that gives great tips for helping couples communicate better and transform their marriage.

~ **Julie Baumgardner**, MS, CFLE, president and executive
director of First Things First

I cannot think of a more critical area to focus the power of coaching than on marriages. Alan and Autumn Ray understand coaching and have provided a helpful guide on how to apply coaching effectively within a marriage so the marriage partners can be a more successful team. If you want to be part of a winning marriage team, look to the power of coaching and to this simply effective book as a valuable resource.

~ **Chad Hall**, director of coaching, Western Seminary

Rick and Jane Learn to Listen and Talk: The First Step to Intimacy by Alan and Autumn Ray pleasantly surprised me. When I heard that the book was written in the style of a first grade reader, my first thought was "You've got to be kidding!" But the book really does communicate in a non-technical way to anyone who wants to develop better communication, especially through a team coaching platform.

~ **Terry Northcut**t, director, Marriage Enrichment Programs,
Family Dynamics Institute

Simple, yet profound truths you can apply today. That's what Rick and Jane Learn to Listen and Talk provides. A quick investment with a big benefit.

~ **Ron L. Deal**, co-author of The Remarriage Checkup

FOREWORD

The purpose of this book is threefold. First, it introduces coaching as an effective approach to strengthen marriages. Second, it provides the basic tools for improved communication. Third, it introduces the concept that marriages are like teams that can be strengthened when both teammates play from a common playbook. This team concept is powerful.

Marriage fits the definition of a team well. A team is a group working together trying to achieve common goals using common processes. In marriage, there is a group of two trying to work together to achieve common goals (happiness, health, raising good kids, a nice retirement, etc.). What often is missing is the common process or a common playbook.

The narrative captures the essence of MarriageTeam's[1] first coaching session on communication. Basic communication skills are presented, applied, and reinforced throughout the coaching process as Rick and Jane work through the issues they are facing.

While the skills themselves are simple, it is often difficult to implement them, because emotions get in the way. Marriage coaches have a significant impact as Rick and

---

[1] MarriageTeam is a nonprofit organization that trains Christian couples to be marriage coaches and places couples wanting to improve their marriage with these coaches. More information is available at www.MarriageTeam.org.

Jane learn and practice the new skills. We hope you enjoy watching this process unfold and use these insights to create your own winning marriage.

ACKNOWLEDGEMENTS

We want to thank the many coaches and couples who have shared their lives with us through the coaching process. The insights and coaching techniques outlined here were developed through their hard work, sweat, and tears (no blood, to the best of our knowledge).

If there is anything we have learned in coaching couples, it is that having a good marriage is a journey. We never arrive at our final destination, as there are always new challenges and issues. We have found that with a common playbook, our team is better able to play the game of married life together and experience the thrill of victory.

DEDICATION

This book is dedicated to our parents, Walt and Marion Ray and Jim and Mary Lois Peters, who had life-long marriages. While no marriage is perfect, our parents gave us the gift of playbooks without a divorce play, which made it psychologically more difficult for us to consider that option when things were tough.

It didn't seem like much of a gift at the time we were married, but in retrospect, it was the best gift ever.

Our hope is that in some small way, this book will help you leave a similar legacy of an enduring marriage to your children. If you have already experienced a divorce, we hope this book will encourage you. While we cannot undo the past, we can create a new legacy with the actions we take today.

TABLE OF CONTENTS

Rick and Jane's Wedding Day
(three years ago)

Chapter 1 – Rick and Jane Fight

Jane is quiet.

Rick asks, "What is wrong?"

Jane says, "Nothing."

Rick insists something is wrong.

Jane will not talk.

Rick gets mad.

See Rick and Jane fight.

Fight, fight, fight.

Rick yells at Jane.

Jane cries and goes to her room.

Rick and Jane have a dog.

Her name is Dot.

Dot runs when Rick and Jane fight.

Run, Dot, run!

No one talks for the rest of the day.

DISAGREEMENTS ARE INEVITABLE
BUT THE SILENT TREATMENT,
OR WORSE, IS NOT.

Rick and Jane are fighting again.

The next day, Jane tells her friend, Carol, about the fight.

Jane says it was a silly fight.

"Rick does not understand me.

If Rick loved me, he would know what is wrong."

Jane cries again.

Jane asks Carol, "What can I do?"

Jane talks with Carol.

Carol remembers her fights with Bob before marriage coaching.

Carol understands.

Carol asks, "Jane, do you want to hear a story?"

Jane says, "Sure."

Carol says, "Marriage is like being on a team.

Each of you was born into a different team or family.

Each learned 'plays' to get along on the team.

One team may have been better at winning than the other.

That is normal.

You both grew up.

Each of you wanted a team of your own.

You found Rick.

You married Rick.

You formed your own marriage team."

MARRIAGE IS A TEAM EFFORT.

Carol continues, "There is one BIG problem.

Rick brought his playbook.

You brought your playbook.

You did not share playbooks.

If you were a football team, it would be like this.

You say, 'Go down and in and I will pass the ball there.'

Rick has always run down and out so that is what he hears.

You throw the ball, but Rick is not there.

The pass is incomplete."

Jane throws the ball down and in while Rick
is down and out in more ways than one.

"Both of you are mad.

Both of you are frustrated.

Rick blames you.

You blame Rick.

No one is scoring.

Your team is losing.

If you find another team, you still have the same problem of different playbooks."

THE PROBLEM IS NOT
YOUR TEAMMATE; IT IS
THE DIFFERENT PLAYBOOKS.

Jane listens thoughtfully.

"Carol, you are right.

Rick will understand this.

What should we do?"

Jane asks Carol for advice.

Carol and Bob have completed marriage coaching.

She knows coaches do not give advice.

Carol wisely asks, "What are you willing to do?"

Jane says, "Anything it takes."

Carol says, "That is good.

Change is hard work.

Our marriage coach couple helped us create a common playbook."

TEAM PERFORMANCE IS ENHANCED
WITH COACHING

Rick listens to Jane.

Chapter 2 – The Decision for Coaching

Jane tells Carol's story to Rick.

Rick listens.

He remembers high school football.

He was the quarterback but changed schools sophomore year.

He had to learn all new plays. It was hard work, but the work paid off.

Rick and his new team had a winning season.

Rick is tired of fighting.

Rick does not like losing.

Rick and Jane decide to try coaching.

But Rick and Jane are nervous.

They don't know what to expect.

Will they have to "tell all"?

Jane asks Rick, "What do we have to lose?"

Rick replies, "Not much. I do not like the way things are now.

Let's just do it!!"

Let's just do it!

Rick reads about marriage coaching and calls for more information.

A marriage coach answers all his questions.

Rick and Jane are happy to know that coaches only focus on what Rick and Jane want to discuss.

Rick and Jane sign up.

They each complete an online inventory called ENRICH.

A marriage coach explains how it will help make their team a winning team.

Soon they meet with their coach couple, Sam and Sally.

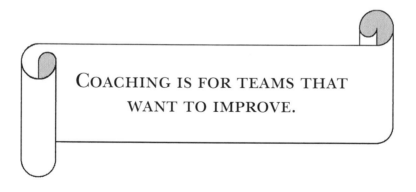

COACHING IS FOR TEAMS THAT
WANT TO IMPROVE.

Rick and Jane meet their coaches.

Chapter 3 – Meeting the Coaches

Rick and Jane go to their coaches' home.

Sam and Sally welcome Rick and Jane.

Together they sit around the dining room table.

Sam gives Rick and Jane their *Player Workbooks* with the skill building and awareness exercises they will be using over the next several weeks.

Sam tells Rick and Jane about the coaching process, ground rules, and other details.

He takes some notes so he can do a better job of coaching.

He tells about a place in their workbooks to take notes on key points and agreements.

Sally tells them how glad she and Sam are that Rick and Jane have decided to be coached.

Coaching begins.

Sam and Sally share how they met at school.

Sam says their marriage has not always been as good as it is now.

Sally says some very dear friends divorced and they wanted to help them, but did not know how.

Sam and Sally decided to learn about coaching so they could help in the future.

Now their marriage is even better and they enjoy helping others.

MARRIAGE COACHES ARE ORDINARY COUPLES WHO LEARN COACHING SKILLS TO HELP OTHER MARRIAGES.

Sam asks Rick and Jane how they met.

Rick and Jane talk about their early years together.

Jane tells about how Rick proposed.

Rick and Jane have been married for three years.

Jane says, "We just knew we were meant for each other, but now I'm not as sure."

Sam and Sally smile and tell about their doubts after only six months.

Rick and Jane having fun on their date.

Rick thinks to himself, "Coaching doesn't seem so bad."

Jane thinks, "Sam and Sally seem to really care about us."

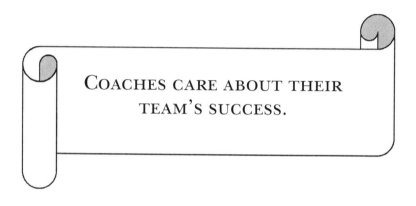

COACHES CARE ABOUT THEIR
TEAM'S SUCCESS.

Jane talking to Rick and Rick feeling attacked.

Chapter 4 – Goals and the Side Track

Sally asks, "What do you want to accomplish with coaching?"

Rick talks.

Jane talks.

They both talk at once.

Sam politely stops them.

He explains that both of them talking at the same time is a bad play.

He asks why that might be.

Both Rick and Jane start to reply, but realize what they have done.

Jane goes first, "I guess if we both are talking, no one is listening."

Rick agrees and adds, "We do that a lot."

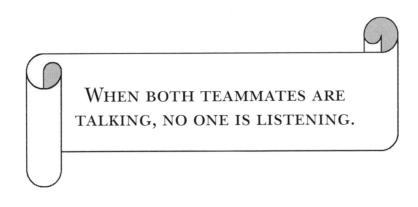

WHEN BOTH TEAMMATES ARE TALKING, NO ONE IS LISTENING.

Sally explains that two great plays for a winning team are effective speaking and active listening.

Sally says, "The goal of talking is to communicate.

However, when our teammate senses an attack, effective communication breaks down."

Sally asks Jane if she can think of a time when that happened on her team.

Jane replies, "Yes, it happens a lot."

Sally asks for a specific example.

Jane says, "I will point out that Rick did not take out the garbage like he said—

Rick jumps in and says, "You say it with an angry tone and—"

Sam again politely stops the conversation.

He asks Rick and Jane if they realize what just happened.

Rick quickly replies, "Yes, she just attacked me once again—"

Before Rick finishes his sentence, Jane jumps in, "I didn't attack you, I just—"

Once again, Sam stops the conversation.

He observes, "Rick and Jane, you have both tried to talk over each other twice in the last thirty seconds."

He then asks, "How is this play working for you?"

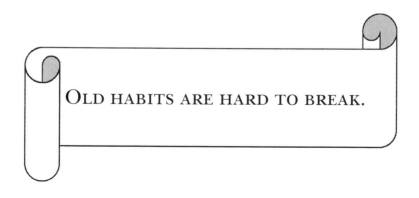

OLD HABITS ARE HARD TO BREAK.

Rick and Jane pause and look a little downcast.

Rick replies, "It is not working well.

I guess that is why we came for coaching."

Jane replies to Rick, "So you do not like the way we talk to each other either?"

Rick replies, "No, I don't."

Jane responds, "Wow, I thought it was just me."

Sally exclaims, "Congratulations, you did it!"

Both Rick and Jane look surprised, and together they ask, "Did what?"

Jane listens to Rick.

Sally says that Rick finished his sentence and Jane listened enough to be able to understand what he said and verify it with him.

She says, "You were taking the first steps to actively listen."

She asks them how that play felt.

Both Rick and Jane laugh.

Rick says, "It felt pretty good.

It almost felt like we were on the same team."

Jane agrees, "I wish we felt that way all the time."

Sam and Sally tell them, "Once you begin using better plays, you will get more winning results."

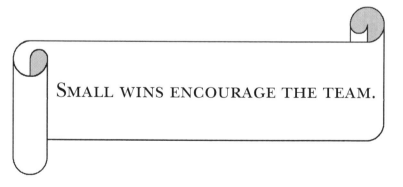

SMALL WINS ENCOURAGE THE TEAM.

Sam summarizes what just happened.

"We took a side trip to focus on communication when it came up.

Communication is the topic for our first meeting.

We will discuss communication in more detail in a minute, but right now let's finish our earlier discussion."

Rick and Jane take a side track.

As a good coach, Sam takes Rick and Jane back to the question that started the side track, "What do you want to accomplish with coaching?"

This time they both think and Jane says to Rick, "You go first."

Rick says, "I want to stop fighting and feel appreciated."

Coach Sally asks, "Is there more?"

Rick responds, "If we could accomplish that it would be huge.

It would be an eleven on a scale of one to ten."

Rick and Jane see themselves reaching their goal.

Sally asks, "How will you know when your goal is accomplished?

What will it specifically look like?"

This is a tough question. Rick thinks and says, "If we had only one fight every couple of weeks that would be a big improvement."

Jane agrees with Rick's goal because it applies to her as well.

She adds, "I want to be able to spend more quality time together as a couple.

It seems like we have become disconnected."

Rick agrees, but notes that it is difficult with their two jobs.

Sally asks Jane how she will know when her goal has been achieved.

Jane replies, "If we had a long weekend together every couple of months that would be great."

COMMON GOALS BRING
TEAMMATES TOGETHER.

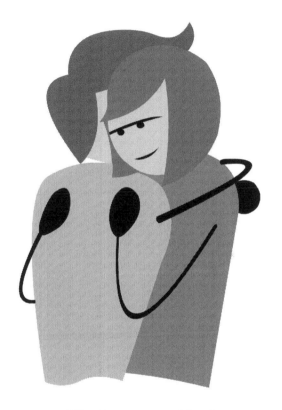

That's a great idea!

Rick and Jane nod in agreement.

Chapter 5 – Effective Speaking

Sally now explains that effective communication occurs when each person feels understood.

"Remember, the desire of the speaker is to be heard and understood.

When our teammate senses an attack, he or she wants to fight back and does not actively listen."

Sally reminds them how that played out a few minutes ago.

Rick and Jane both nod. They understand.

Sam states, "There are *job descriptions* for both the speaker and the listener."

Sally says the key to effective speaking is using an "I" statement when you have emotions about a situation and explains:

Begin by saying 'I.'

Own and state your feelings.

Describe the behavior or situation causing your feelings. Do not use 'you.'

Explain how the behavior or situation impacts you.

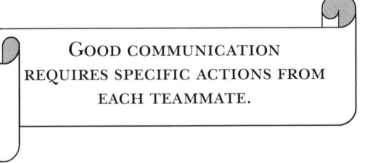

GOOD COMMUNICATION
REQUIRES SPECIFIC ACTIONS FROM
EACH TEAMMATE.

Rick and Jane have new job descriptions.

Sam says, "For example, let's go back to the discussion about taking out the garbage.

Jane, what are you feeling when Rick forgets to take out the garbage?"

Jane thinks for a minute and replies, "I guess I am feeling disappointed that Rick did not do what he promised."

Sam asks, "So how would you put that in an 'I' statement?"

Jane says, "I am disappointed when you don't take out the garbage because I am trying to get dinner and have to stop to do it."

Sam replies, "That is pretty good, but you used a 'you' when you described the behavior.

How could you say it differently?"

Jane thinks and tries again.

I could say, "When the garbage is not taken out."

Sam asks, "So what is the whole 'I' statement?"

Jane answers, "I am disappointed when the garbage doesn't get taken out because I am trying to get dinner and have to stop to do it."

Sam says, "Great.

The change is subtle, but very important.

Both of you know who didn't take out the garbage, but it does not sound like an attack."

Sally asks Rick and Jane, "What makes this a good play?"

Together they ponder this question and come up with:

- It is hard to argue about what your teammate is feeling.

- Our feelings are valid for each of us.

- The speaker takes responsibility for his or her feelings.

- There is no attack on the other teammate.

- Describing what has happened from the speaker's perspective gives the other teammate a broader understanding of the situation.

- Sharing the personal impact helps one teammate empathize more with the other.

Rick talks and Jane agrees.

They pause for a moment to think if there are any other factors.

Finally, Rick exclaims, "I get it! If I don't feel attacked and understand what has just happened to my teammate, I will be more likely to want to help her."

Jane adds, "If I were to hear all that from Rick, I would be motivated to be his teammate and work together with him as well."

Jane talks and Rick agrees.

Sam and Sally both exclaim together, "Wow!"

Sally continues, "You both got it.

That was easy, wasn't it?"

Rick and Jane are not so sure.

Jane says, "I think it will take a lot of practice."

Rick agrees.

Sam says, "That is why you have a teammate to help you."

He gives Rick and Jane a simple formula for effective speaking when one of them has some emotion around an issue,

> "Start with '**I**.'
>
> State your specific **feelings**.
>
> Describe the behavior or situation without using any 'you's.
>
> Explain the **impact**."

Sam says, "It might be easy to remember '**I FBI**'...
(*I, feeling, behavior, impact*)."

THE DESIRE OF THE SPEAKER IS
TO BE UNDERSTOOD.

Jane scratches her head thinking for an answer.

Chapter 6 – The Dynamic Play

A good coach helps the team create mutual accountability for change.

Sam asks Jane, "If you forget to use an 'I' statement, what can Rick say or do to encourage you to use an 'I' statement ...without making you mad?"

No one has asked Jane this question before, and she is stumped.

Sam waits for her reply.

Jane says, "I don't know."

Sam asks her, "If you don't know, who will know?"

Jane has to admit that no one else will.

It is up to her.

Sam repeats the question, "If you forget to use an 'I' statement when you have some emotion around an issue, what can Rick say or do to encourage you to use an 'I' statement...without making you mad?"

Jane says, "I guess Rick could say, 'I really want to help you.

Would you use an 'I' statement to tell me what you are feeling?'"

Sam says, "Great.

Write that down on a three by five card.

We call that a 'dynamic play.'"

Dynamic Play: When Jane forgets to use an "I" statement, Rick will say:

I really want to help you. Would you use an 'I" statement to tell me what you are feeling?

Sally tells Jane to give the card to Rick.

Sally tells Rick the reason for the card.

"It is unlikely you will remember those words because the words are Jane's.

The card is your play to work with Jane so you both get a win."

Home Team scores!

The coaches have Rick read the play back to Jane to see if it really does sound encouraging to her.

Rick reads, "I really want to help you. Would you use an 'I' statement to tell me what you are feeling?"

Jane smiles.

She thinks this play will encourage her to use "I" statements if she forgets.

Rick reads the new, dynamic play (Jane's words) to Jane.

The coaches repeat the process with Rick.

Rick's words are, "Honey, remember that we agreed to use 'I' statements."

He writes his words on a 3x5 card and gives it to Jane.

Jane reads the play to Rick and he confirms it still sounds good when Jane says it.

Now, Jane knows what words will encourage Rick and will not make him mad.

Both teammates are excited to have a new play for their playbook.

Dynamic Play: When Rick forgets to use an "I" statement, Jane will say:

Honey, remember that we agreed to use "I" statements.

Jane asks, "What if our dynamic plays do not work?"

Sam replies, "That sometimes happens.

What do you think you can do?"

Jane thinks for a moment, and then says, "I guess we can change the words and try again."

Sam confirms that many couples do that.

Sally asks if there are more options.

Rick says, "We could take a time out."

Jane agrees.

Sally says, "There are many options.

The key is each teammate's willingness to try new plays if an old one does not work.

After all, you are on the same team, and losing is no fun."

How to Create a Dynamic Play

Ask Yourself

WHEN I FORGET TO _____, WHAT
CAN MY TEAMMATE SAY OR DO TO
ENCOURAGE ME TO DO WHAT
I AGREED I WANT TO DO?

(WRITE IT DOWN. GIVE IT TO YOUR
TEAMMATE.)

Rick and Jane rate their listening skills.

Chapter 7 – Active Listening

Sam asks, "What else, aside from a speaker, is needed for communication to occur?"

Jane answers, "Someone needs to listen."

Sally explains, "The basic job description of the listener is to ensure the speaker feels understood.

Remember, understanding someone does not mean agreeing with him!"

Sam emphasizes that the listener does not have to agree with the speaker for the speaker to feel understood.

Sam asks both Rick and Jane to rate their listening skills on a self assessment.

(You can also rate your listening skills on the "Self Assessment." Two extra self assessments are at the back of the book.)

My Listening Skills
Self Assessment

Good Active Listening Behaviors	1 Almost Never	2 Not Much	3 Some-times	4 Often	5 Almost Always
1. I listen without criticizing.					
2. I listen without prejudging.					
3. I listen without being defensive.					
4. I listen without giving advice unless asked.					
5. I listen without thinking about a reply.					
6. I let my teammate complete his/her sentences.					
7. I let my teammate finish before I talk.					
8. I try to understand my teammate's feelings.					
9. I look at my teammate while I listen.					
10. I give full attention when my teammate speaks.					
11. I try to understand my teammate's viewpoint.					
12. I look for my teammate's non-verbal messages.					
13. I repeat back my understanding of what my teammate said, in both content and feelings.					
14. I ask, "Did I understand you correctly?" and wait for a reply.					
15. I ask, "Is there more?" after my teammate finishes talking.					

Sam asks Rick what he learned from the self assessment.

Rick replies, "I thought I was a pretty good listener until I did this assessment, but now I don't think so."

Sally asks Jane the same question.

Jane agrees with Rick, "I thought my listening was better than it appears to be."

Sally says, "The self assessment is the first step to improving your listening. If you do not know your weaknesses, how can you improve?"

WHILE WE MAY "KNOW" MANY GOOD LISTENING BEHAVIORS, WE OFTEN DO NOT APPLY THEM WITH OUR TEAMMATE.

Sally says that the skills listed in the self assessment are the job description of a good listener.

Rick comments, "That is a pretty demanding job description."

They all agree.

Sam asks, "What would motivate you to improve your listening skills?"

Rick says, "Better communication motivates me. I am tired of arguing with Jane. If changing the way I listen will help, count me in."

Jane says, "I think I need to be a better listener, too. I also am tired of the arguments."

Rick and Jane nod in agreement.

Sally asks Jane, "What two listening skills would most improve your communication if Rick were to regularly use them?"

Jane studies the list carefully and replies, "I would like Rick to listen without becoming defensive (#3) and really try to understand my feelings (#8)."

Now it is Rick's turn and he says, "I would like Jane to give her full attention to me when I speak (#10) and try to understand my viewpoint (#11)."

Rick and Jane select new listening
skills for each other to use.

Sam asks if the team is ready to accept the "listening challenge."

Rick and Jane look quizzically at each other.

Sam asks, "Rick, for this next week, will you agree to do numbers three and eight for Jane?"

Rick replies that he will.

Sam then asks Jane if she will do numbers ten and eleven for Rick.

Jane agrees as well.

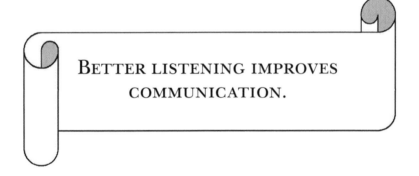

BETTER LISTENING IMPROVES COMMUNICATION.

Sally continues, "Sometimes it is hard to remember new behaviors.

Jane, if you forget to use your new skills and revert to old listening patterns, how would you like Rick to remind you to use your new skills?"

Jane can see another dynamic play coming.

She thinks for a minute and says, "I would like Rick to say, 'I really like it when we use our new listening skills.'"

She then writes a play card.

They check it out, with Rick reading the card to Jane.

Jane confirms that hearing it is encouraging to her.

**Dynamic Play: When Jane forgets to use
the new listening skills, Rick will say:**

I really like it when we use our new listening skills.

Rick writes the words that he needs to hear to remind him to use both of his new listening behaviors.

His first play is, "Honey, I know we both want better communication. Will you try not to be defensive?"

His second play is, "Honey, I know we both want better communication. Will you try to understand my feelings?"

Dynamic Plays: When Rick becomes defensive, Jane will say:

Honey, I know we both want better communication. Will you try not to be defensive?

Dynamic Plays: When Rick forgets to listen for Jane's feelings, Jane will say:

Honey, I know we both want
better communication.
Will you try to understand
my feelings?

Rick and Jane are on the same team
with some new plays.

Chapter 8 – The Wrap-Up

Sam asks, "What do you both think about your new plays?"

Rick answers first, "They seem pretty simple now.

I just hope they are that simple to use when we need them."

Before anyone can say anything, Rick quickly adds, "Yea, I know that is why I have a teammate to help me."

Jane says, "I am pretty excited about having a game plan to try something different.

I really hate the way we have been talking to each other."

Sally concludes, "You have both done some good work and we look forward to hearing how your communication is this coming week."

They all rise from the table.

Sam and Sally talk with Rick and Jane as they rise from the table.

As they walk to the door, Rick and Jane thank Sam and Sally for their time and hospitality.

As they drive away, Rick says, "That wasn't so bad. I'm glad Carol told you about marriage coaching."

Jane replies, "I am too."

Jane continues, "We covered a lot and I would like to review our notes tomorrow so we don't forget anything.

Can we do that?"

Rick replies, "That is a great idea.

Let's do it after dinner."

Rick and Jane say goodbye to Sam and Sally.

The next day, after dinner, Rick and Jane review their *Player Workbooks.*

They compare notes and make a list of what they learned.

- Disagreements are inevitable but the silent treatment, or worse, is not.

- Marriage is a team effort.

- The problem is not the teammates; it is the different playbooks.

- Team performance is enhanced with coaching.

- Coaching is for teams that want to improve.

- Marriage coaches are ordinary couples who learn coaching skills to help other marriages.

- Coaches care about their team's success.

- When both teammates are talking, no one is listening.

- Old habits are hard to break.

- Small wins encourage the team.

- Common goals bring teammates together.

- Good communication requires specific actions from each teammate.

- The desire of the speaker is to be understood.

- While we may "know" many good listening behaviors, we often don't apply them with our teammate.

- Better listening improves communication.

The speaker's job is to use an "I" statement when emotions are involved.

- Start with **"I."**
- Identify your **Feelings**.
- Describe the behavior or situation without using any 'you's.
- Explain the **Impact**.
- Remember **I FBI**.

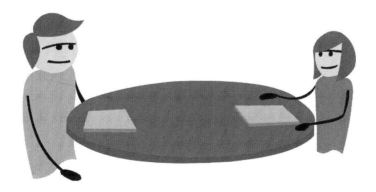

Rick and Jane review their new plays.

The Listener's job is to ensure the speaker feels understood.

- Listen without criticizing.

- Listen without prejudging.

- Listen without being defensive.

- Listen without giving advice unless asked.

- Listen without thinking about a reply.

- Let my teammate complete his/her sentences.

- Let my teammate finish before I talk.

- Try to understand my teammate's feelings.

- Look at my teammate while I listen.

- Give full attention when my teammate speaks.

- Try to understand my teammate's viewpoint.

- Look for my teammate's non-verbal messages.

- Repeat back my understanding of what my teammate said, in both content and feelings.

- Ask, "Did I understand you correctly?" and wait for a reply.

- Ask, "Is there more?" after my teammate finishes talking.

Finally, Rick and Jane layout their dynamic plays.

Dynamic Play: When Jane forgets to use an "I" statement, Rick will say:

I really want to help you. Would you use an "I" statement to tell me what you are feeling?

Dynamic Play: When Rick forgets to use an "I" statement, Jane will say:

Honey, remember that we agreed to use "I" statements.

Dynamic Play: When Jane forgets to use the new listening skills, Rick will say:

I really like it when we use our new listening skills.

Jane has two different plays where she says Rick's words to Rick.

Dynamic Play: When Rick becomes defensive, Jane will say:

Honey, I know we both want better communication. Will you try not to be defensive?

Dynamic Play: When Rick forgets to listen for Jane's feelings, Jane will say:

> Honey, I know we both want
> better communication.
> Will you try to understand
> my feelings?

Rick summarizes how to create a dynamic play.

When one of us forgets to do <u>something we agreed to do</u>,

- We need to ask ourselves, "What can my teammate say or do to encourage me to do what I agreed I want to do?"

- We then need to write it down and give it to our teammate for a new team play.

When they finish, Jane is first to speak.

"That is quite a list we learned last night."

Rick agrees and adds, "Not only that, but I had a good time with Sam and Sally."

Jane replies, "I like Sam and Sally and look forward to developing more new plays. They said our next session will help us learn about our anger."

Rick says, "I am really looking forward to that."

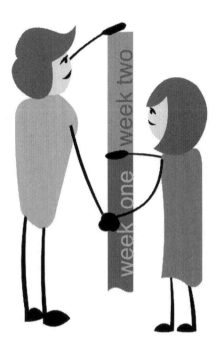

Rick and Jane measure how much their relationship has grown.

CHAPTER 9 – THE TEAM CHALLENGE

Rick and Jane are still sitting at the dining room table.

Rick has an idea.

"I'll bet readers are thinking, 'Nice story, but it seems too simple to work.'"

Jane looks puzzled, "Sooo...?"

Rick goes on, "We can challenge them to apply 'I' statements and active listening for a week and let us know how they work."

Jane catches the idea and continues, "Great idea! They can even create their own dynamic plays and share them with us on our Facebook page: www.facebook.com/RickandJane or email us at rickandjane@marriageteam.org."

Rick now has another idea.

"As a reminder to ourselves, we can create a couple of posters to hang in the house so we don't forget to use "I" statements and active listening."

Jane agrees to create the posters.

She says, "We can post them on www.MarriageTeam.org/RnJPoster.html as a FREE DOWNLOAD for our readers."

Rick smiles at Jane and says, "We DO make a good team!"

Jane smiles at Rick and says, "Let's go to bed early and practice our new communication skills."

Rick and Jane go to bed early to practice their communication.

The next book in the *Learn to be Married Series for Rick and Jane* is:

**Rick and Jane Learn to
Use Anger Creatively**

My Listening Skills
Self Assessment

Good Active Listening Behaviors	1 Almost Never	2 Not Much	3 Some-times	4 Often	5 Almost Always
1. I listen without criticizing.					
2. I listen without prejudging.					
3. I listen without being defensive.					
4. I listen without giving advice unless asked.					
5. I listen without thinking about a reply.					
6. I let my teammate complete his/her sentences.					
7. I let my teammate finish before I talk.					
8. I try to understand my teammate's feelings.					
9. I look at my teammate while I listen.					
10. I give full attention when my teammate speaks.					
11. I try to understand my teammate's viewpoint.					
12. I look for my teammate's non-verbal messages.					
13. I repeat back my understanding of what my teammate said, in both content and feelings.					
14. I ask, "Did I understand you correctly?" and wait for a reply.					
15. I ask, "Is there more?" after my teammate finishes talking.					

My Listening Skills
Self Assessment

Good Active Listening Behaviors	1 Almost Never	2 Not Much	3 Some-times	4 Often	5 Almost Always
1. I listen without criticizing.					
2. I listen without prejudging.					
3. I listen without being defensive.					
4. I listen without giving advice unless asked.					
5. I listen without thinking about a reply.					
6. I let my teammate complete his/her sentences.					
7. I let my teammate finish before I talk.					
8. I try to understand my teammate's feelings.					
9. I look at my teammate while I listen.					
10. I give full attention when my teammate speaks.					
11. I try to understand my teammate's viewpoint.					
12. I look for my teammate's non-verbal messages.					
13. I repeat back my understanding of what my teammate said, in both content and feelings.					
14. I ask, "Did I understand you correctly?" and wait for a reply.					
15. I ask, "Is there more?" after my teammate finishes talking.					

ABOUT THE AUTHORS

Al and Autumn are the co-founders of MarriageTeam, a nonprofit organization that trains Christian couples to be marriage coaches and places couples with coaches. The MarriageTeam vision is to have marriage coach couples around the country actively living out their faith by strengthening and saving marriages as an outreach to the community.

If you would like to learn more about how you can start a MarriageTeam coaching capability in your community, give MarriageTeam a call.

MarriageTeam
1400 NE 136th Ave
Vancouver, WA 98684
PO Box 873086
Vancouver, WA 98687-3086
info@marriageteam.org
www.marriageteam.org
360 450-6042
866 831-4201

You Can Make a Difference

MarriageTeam exists to strengthen marriages, reduce divorce, and thereby create stronger families. Virtually everyone has been touched by the divorce of a loved one. You can make a difference by:

- Becoming a <u>monthly</u> partner with **your contributions**.
- Making a one-time donation.
- **Talking with your pastor** about having trained marriage coaches in your church and community.
- Getting additional information from MarriageTeam. We have Skype coaching available.

MarriageTeam is a Washington State non-profit recognized by the IRS as a tax exempt, public charity according to IRS Code, Section 501(c)(3).

You can donate to MarriageTeam by:

- Writing a check or
- Making an on-line donation through our secure Pay Trace partner accessed through http://www.marriageteam.org/Donations.html

DETACH AND RETURN

NAME		
ADDRESS		
CITY	STATE	ZIP
PHONE	E-MAIL	

☐   I would like to make a donation of $_____per_____

All donations are tax deductible. We will send a receipt. Thank you.

Send your donations to: **MarriageTeam,**
P.O. Box 873086,
Vancouver, WA 98687

7963315R0

Made in the USA
Charleston, SC
26 April 2011